Studies in

CHRISTIAN HIGHER EDUCATION

Number 6

Studies in Christian Higher Education

Number 1: *Problems in College Administration* by A. J. Brumbaugh

Number 2: *Building a Faculty in a Church-Related College of Liberal Arts* by Clarence E. Ficken

Number 3: *The Education of the Administrator* by Goodrich C. White

Number 4: *An Experiment in General Education* by William E. Kerstetter and Phillips Moulton

Number 5: *Handbook for Trustees* by Myron F. Wicke

Number 6: *On Teaching in a Christian College* by Myron F. Wicke

ON TEACHING
IN A
CHRISTIAN COLLEGE

On Teaching in a Christian College

by
MYRON F. WICKE
Dean of Arts and Sciences
Southwestern University

1961
DIVISION OF HIGHER EDUCATION
Board of Education, The Methodist Church
Nashville, Tennessee

Issued by
Director of Information and Publications
DIVISION OF HIGHER EDUCATION
Board of Education, The Methodist Church
P. O. Box 871, Nashville 2, Tennessee

To

faculty and students

of

Southwestern of Texas

whose spirit and understanding have made

work with them a joy

and to

William C. Finch

Southwestern's president 1950-1961

who exemplifies the Christian educator.

Preface

In these days when church-related educational institutions are asking about the definition of the Christian college, it is well to remember that Christian is the adjective which modifies college. Its meaning as a modifier depends entirely on the worthiness of the image formed in the mind of people who hear it applied. A college which calls itself Christian is a vulnerable one. Its shortcomings will be magnified by critics who expect of Christian institutions something special.

No group associated with a college is more influential in creating an image in the public mind than the faculty. If teachers act upon the belief that Christianity has relevance to what they say and teach, the alumni will reflect this same sympathetic attitude. If teachers reflect the Christian way, this will not mean that the religious atmosphere of the college will be oppressive or that the freedom of teachers will be restricted.

When the Christian church moves to strengthen the tie with Christian institutions of higher learning, it projects a double-edged program. The college can meet the church's challenge only by seriously striving to create the sort of atmosphere in which Christian ideals may live and grow. This volume was prepared by one who believes that when good teaching and Christian idealism are united, both the spiritual and scholarly efforts are reinforced.

JOHN O. GROSS
Nashville, Tennessee
March 10, 1961

WE SHOULD pray for colleges because in so doing we pray for everything else. In the present members of our colleges we have the future teachers and rulers of our nation—the professional men and men of influence of the coming generation—the rising hope of our country, the Church, and the world. In praying for them, therefore, we pray for our country in its magistrates, for the Church in its ministers, for the world in its missionaries, for every good cause in its future agents and representatives, for all the streams of influence in their foundation and their source.

W. S. TYLER
in *Prayers for Colleges*
published in 1855

Contents

I

The Profession

THE PROFESSION of teaching is one of the oldest, and is today in the United States the largest in point of numbers. It is estimated that there were more than one million teachers in the United States in 1956, or roughly one for each 165 persons in the nation. About one tenth of these teachers were in college or university work.

Teaching is a learned profession with its own peculiar and essential demands. Teaching is one aspect of education which can be discussed in concrete terms. While "education" is abstract, "teaching" is practical. We should doubtless all be better off if we talked less about "education" and thought more about teaching.

Teaching as a Learned Profession

The three original learned professions were theology, law, and medicine. Today numerous other human endeavors are properly considered as professions in their own right.

It is instructive to examine the origin of the word "profession." To profess meant to confess, to declare openly a position on a matter of importance. Unfortunately the history of words is that they more often deteriorate than improve in connotation. There are now unpleasant as well as positive overtones to the term "professional." At times "to profess" is taken to imply public statement of faith without actual belief or practice. Thus the English poet Cowper said of some: "So little felt, so fervently professed." The related word "professional" also has unpleasant connotations. To be a "professional patriot" is to be one who feels little love of country while still prating about the depth of his patriotism.

A learned profession is one which requires knowledge and skill of a high order. The teacher in his vocation professes faith in the use of the intelligence to guide and enrich the personality and spirit. To be successful the teacher must, in other words, believe that teaching can make a difference.

Some Marks of a Learned Profession

The marks of a learned profession have been variously characterized. President John S. Millis of Western Reserve University suggests as fundamental the following distinctions which are here paraphrased:

1. *The learned profession requires judgment.*[1]

   Until human judgment has been exercised, professional skills are of no use. Judgment must be acquired. It cannot be taught except in the narrowest of limits.

2. *The learned profession requires multidisciplinary learning.*

   Competence in teaching requires abilities and

---

[1] John S. Millis, "Educating Teachers as Professionals," *The Journal of Higher Education* (Columbus, Ohio: Ohio State University Press, April, 1957), pp. 179-185.

understanding in a broad area. Teachers must, therefore, be liberally trained. They must continue to expand the area of their understanding.

3. *The learned profession deals directly with people.* Understanding of individual human beings is essential to the teacher. Unless he believes that the student is of first importance in the educational process, and that he can change, the teacher's work is likely to prove ineffective.
4. *The learned profession links knowledge and skill inseparably.*

   Teaching is thus an applied art. When seen as less than an art, it becomes subject-centered, often pedantic, and relatively ineffective.

Any close examination of these characteristics of the learned profession will reveal how demanding they are. Knowledge is required—broad knowledge. But an understanding of human beings and a skill in meeting their needs are also essential. Every teacher will profit from a continuing review of his development in the light of these standards.

Growth in the Profession Since knowledge increases constantly, the practitioner of a learned profession must by definition grow in knowledge. This means as a minimum that the teacher must follow disciplined plans to study both his own and other fields. If such plans are not carried out with diligence and dedication, the teacher is sure to find himself lost in an academic lock step, and in time he will become discouraged and disgruntled. Keeping intellectually and spiritually alive is the major requirement.

It is at this point, of course, that the dignity of the profession is most at stake. Many young people enter teaching careers with high ideals and bright hopes. As they discover the magnitude of their task, and the obstacles in their path, placed there by circumstances and at times by thoughtless administrators, some gradually succumb to a lower view of teaching. In their surrender, the profession loses much of its power and dignity. Of course, no one ought to expect the dignity of the profession to support his performance; rather the performance must support the dignity of the profession. Teachers grow or decay. There is hardly a middle ground.

Salaries and Mission It is a commonplace fact that the teacher in America is underpaid. Every responsible college administrator understands this problem, and is doing his best to find solutions. Salaries must advance. Even with more defensible salary scales, however, it is not likely that teaching will ever be among the highest paid of professions. While teachers should not be exploited, as often they are, they will doubtless always be among those whose sense of mission must supply much of their basic motivation.

This sense of mission must be inspired primarily by the knowledge that teaching matters. The teacher teaches the doctor, the lawyer, the preacher, the homemaker. What is more, *the teacher teaches the teacher.* Hence teaching, like a stone dropped into a pool of water, sends impulses into every part of the world's life. Again and again, we hear grateful testimony by the nation's leaders concerning the influence of certain teachers upon them. A leading citizen said recently, "No other profession has the potentialities that college teaching has, and none is less understood and appreciated." [2] Henry Adams has put it more sharply: "A teacher affects eternity. He can never tell where his influence stops."

The Teacher's Future Some of the best teaching is done by young, inexperienced teachers. There are many reasons for this. The young teacher is nearer the age of his students, and he may be more keenly aware of their problems. More important perhaps are the young teacher's enthusiasm for his material, and his youthful vigor.

Many experienced teachers look back longingly to their first years in the classroom. In a recent book by a public-school superintendent, the author insists that if he were sure he could repeat the satisfactions of his first year of teaching, no amount of money or prestige could keep him in administration. He adds this note: "I have found that nine times out of ten, a good beginning teacher makes up for his lack of experience by an almost passionate devotion to his job." [3]

On the other hand, a mature, long-experienced

---

[2] Howard Lowry and William Taeusch, *Research—Creative Activity and Teaching* (New York: The Carnegie Foundation for the Advancement of Teaching, 1953), p. 9.

[3] Charles H. Wilson, *A Teacher Is a Person* (New York: Holt, Rinehart & Winston, Inc., 1956).

teacher who has grown personally and professionally represents the teacher at his very best. The problem is how to continue to grow, from the first days of teaching to the last, even though youthfulness cannot be retained or recaptured. One way is to aim constantly at new and higher goals.

Planning for the Future Nothing is more important to a teacher, therefore, than his personal plans for development in the profession. These should be consciously laid, frequently appraised, and often revised. Since a teacher must be an expert in a field of knowledge, he should determine early how best to keep up to date and to increase his creativity. If he will select early one or two aspects of his field in which to become particularly proficient, he will find the area of his study growing from year to year. Using this material in his classes will enrich his courses greatly. At the same time, brief articles can be planned in these areas, and gradually material for a book or two and for public lectures will take shape.

The experience of a colleague of the writer, an English teacher, will serve as an illustration. In middle age he became greatly interested in the study of the ballads of his state. Since he was also an accomplished musician, literary and musical requirements for successful work in ballads were happily joined. His study enriched his teaching, gave him a field for creative writing, and soon placed him in great demand as a lecturer.

Not all fields are as popular with the public as ballads, but every field presents challenge and opportunity. If from year to year one or more areas, closely related to the major discipline of the professor, are progressively studied, the teacher will find himself increasingly an authority in his field. He will also find enough exciting work to fill several careers.[4]

"Wanted: Professional Teachers." In these words President Henry H. Hill of George Peabody College for Teachers suggests a great social need.[5] The actual danger is described succinctly by Jacques Barzun: "With us, many people who pass as professional teachers are merely connected with education." [6]

---

[4] This point is well elaborated in Gilbert Highet's *The Art of Teaching*.

[5] Henry H. Hill, "Wanted: Professional Teachers," *The Atlantic Monthly*, May, 1960, pp. 37-40.

[6] Jacques Barzun, *Teacher in America* (Boston: Little, Brown & Co., 1945), p. 11.

II

The Teacher Is a Person

IT is hardly possible to overestimate the potential influence of an effective teacher. Testimony on this point is widespread and exciting. Says Houston Peterson in his *Great Teachers:*

> In what autobiography is this (the teacher's) fateful influence not underlined? Recalling his two years at the College of William and Mary, Thomas Jefferson wrote, "It was my good fortune, and *what probably fixed the destiny of my life,* that Dr. William Small of Scotland was then professor of mathematics, a man profound in most of the useful branches of science, with a happy talent of communication, and an enlarged and liberal mind." [1]

This note of commendation by a great man for his teacher is particularly interesting for its references to the "happy talent of communication" and to the "enlarged and liberal mind."

We hear frequently—and tiresomely—of the need for "great personalities" in the classroom. All of us would like to be great personalities, but by definition few of us are. Actually the achievement of excellence in teaching is not limited to any small group of supermen. Excellence is a possibility for men and women who do not feel themselves to be "great" in any dramatic sense.

Nicholas Murray Butler put it well when he said,

[1] Houston Peterson, *Great Teachers* (New Brunswick, N. J.: Rutgers University Press, 1946), XVI. (Italics added.)

"Of great teachers, there are not many born in a generation, and nothing is more certain than that such are born and not made. Of good teachers there are, on the other hand, a fair supply. These are the men and women who, by reason of sound if somewhat partial knowledge, orderly-mindedness, skill in simple and clear presentation, and a gift of sympathy, are able to stimulate youth to study and to think." Good teachers can be made, but they make themselves.

Essentials

What is needed most of all in the teacher is a warm and growing human being, devoted to excellence in himself first of all, but dedicated also to a profession which honors the powers of the mind. The teacher must believe that human beings can change and grow as they exercise their minds on important matters. The teacher is a human being dealing with human beings. He will take pride in the development of those who work with him, and always he will find that he can learn from his students. Paradoxically, his major reward comes when he sees a student transcend his teacher. This has been interestingly put in these words:

> The rarest type of teacher transcends the role of guide. (These) teachers lead their students to a trail they themselves have never trod. . . . Each of us, working at his best, will have a small element of greatness, a bit of vision, to light our teaching and to open up, to some of our students at least, a glimpse of life and knowledge that may be theirs, though it can never be ours.[2]

[2] *Improving College and University Teaching*, "Promised Land," Editorial. Summer 1957, Vol. V, No. 3, p. 59.

All this suggests that a teacher will succeed as he is himself alive and alert, in all ways in which human beings can be alive and alert, learning as he teaches, and learning in order to teach. The best way to make a course relevant, says Gilbert Highet, is for the teacher to be relevant. This is no small order; for it demands far more than a specialized knowledge of a single field of scholarship.

When a teacher goes to seed, in his person or in his intellect, he forfeits his opportunity. From the beginning, therefore, this profession especially requires not only *a* discipline, but *discipline. A teacher must live a planned, examined life*. Perhaps no demand is more inescapable; and none is more difficult, since each of us finds his rut comfortable, and the deeper the rut the more complete the comfort.

A teacher's personal discipline must be continuous and conscious. A well-known, highly successful college president each year wrote out for himself an evaluation of his successes and failures, both personal and public, and each year committed to paper a personal "program" for the year ahead. Even after retirement, he found the inventory and the plan essential. A teacher needs precisely such an evaluation of his work and person, taking account of his health, his mind, his spirit, and his personal relationships. What are some of the fundamental questions in such an examination? Here is a check list, by no means comprehensive but perhaps suggestive:

A PERSONAL CHECK LIST FOR TEACHERS

(With points to be added by the teacher himself)

1. My personal goals have recently been re-examined and restated.
2. I am steadily developing a long-range discipline for my life which is helping me to use time and energy more effectively.
3. I have a carefully worked-out program of wide general reading which takes me outside my field of major study.
4. I have definite, considered plans for work in my academic discipline, and I am doing special studies which will enrich my teaching.
5. I do not neglect my health, and I take time for recreation, relaxation, and regular physical checkups.
6. My life is under such control that I have time for my family and associates.
7. I am trying to become a student of the spirit. I allow time for religious reading, devotions, and worship.
8. I have joined others of the campus in discussions of the religious perspectives of teaching.
9. My faith in the possibilities of formal education is growing.
10. I am studying my teaching techniques, and I use every effective device I know to gain the judgments of those who might help, including my students.
11. I have recently visited the classes of acknowledged master teachers, and I have discussed teaching problems with them.

12. As often as possible, I attend professional meetings where teaching is discussed.
13. I am making efforts to understand my students better, and to plan my teaching so that there is actually an encounter of minds among us.
14. I am growing more successful in getting my students to bear a larger share of the burden of their own education.
15. I am making myself available to students.
16. I am trying to take a positive part in developing a climate of academic excellence on my campus.
17. When I disagree with important campus policy, I seek to discuss the problem dispassionately with those of the faculty or administration who have responsibility in the matter.
18. I try to judge administrative officers by the same standards by which I judge myself.
19. I believe that I should speak my convictions in faculty councils, but also that I must speak responsibly, and with awareness of the complexity of the issues.
20. I take pride in the institution I serve, and I hold myself responsible with others for its growing effectiveness.

There are, to be sure, items which each teacher must add for himself, since only he knows himself. It would appear that if there are too many negative items on the check list, some hard thinking is in order.

Teacher Attitude and Student Progress

A teacher must be judged to a large degree by the

progress of his students. Frequently it is the attitude of the teacher which determines the attitude of the student. A teacher is at his best, according to Harold Taylor, when he approaches students in an attitude of trust and expectancy. Experienced teachers know that they get from their students just about what they expect. The plain fact is that only rarely do we expect enough. In any case, the human product is the issue.

The Teacher as a Leader Many years ago President Meiklejohn of Amherst wrote that the teacher should "stand before his pupils and the community at large as the intellectual leader of his time."

When a teacher accepts fully this concept of his position in the educational spectrum, he becomes immediately the major factor in the educational community. For it must be clear, as has often been pointed out, that the value system of the college is determined mainly by the faculty. Presidents and deans, and of course students, come and go; but the faculty as a group are fortunately more stable and more persistent. Obviously there are in this group the best possibilities for educational statesmanship.

Why is it, then, that so often a teacher will regard himself as a law unto himself, with little willingness to consider the good of the whole community? Only the individual can answer. There may be, nevertheless, more than a little wry truth in the reason given by a dean for leaving this office to return to full-time teaching. His statement was: "I'm tired of trying to solve problems. I want to *become* a problem again." The question is discussed further in a subsequent chapter.

Perhaps the best way to end these brief notes on the teacher as a person is to remember that for good or ill we are inevitably influences upon younger pilgrims on the road. Which of us knows what our students especially require at a given moment? We must content ourselves with being at our best and doing our best.

In a context not confined to the classroom, Albert Schweitzer has written as follows about his personal indebtedness to those who crossed his path:

> One other thing stirs me when I look back at my youthful days—the fact that so many people gave me something or were something to me without knowing it. Such people, with whom I never perhaps exchanged a word, yes, and others about whom I merely heard things by report, had a decisive influence on me; they entered into my life and became powers within me. Much that I should otherwise not have felt so clearly or done so effectively was felt or done as it was, because I stand, as it were, under the sway of these people. Hence I always think that we all live, spiritually, by what others have given us in the significant hours of our life. These significant hours do not announce themselves as coming, but arrive unexpected. Nor do they make a great show of themselves; they pass almost unperceived. Often, indeed, their significance comes home to us first as we look back, just as the beauty of a piece of music or of a landscape often strikes us first in our recollection of it. Much that has become our own in gentleness, modesty, kindness, willingness to forgive, in veracity, loyalty, resignation under suffering, we owe to people in whom we have seen or experienced these virtues at work, sometimes in a great matter, sometimes in a small. A thought which had become act sprang into us like a spark, and lighted a new

> flame within us. . . . If we had before us those who have thus been a blessing to us, and could tell them how it came about, they would be amazed to learn what passed over from their life into ours.[3]

The same point has been put in quite another way by Chancellor Samuel B. Gould, University of California, Santa Barbara:

> Regardless of the subject matter involved, the whole (course) should be surrounded by the aura of (the teacher's) personal values, his personal experience, his own wisdom. There is no way to put these in the curriculum.[4]

Such testimony should give the teacher pause, since he of all people touches the young at a most crucial moment in their lives.

---

[3] Albert Schweitzer, *Memoirs of Childhood and Youth* (New York: The Macmillan Co., 1925), pp. 89-91.

[4] Samuel B. Gould, *Curriculum Planning to Meet Tomorrow's Needs* (Washington, D. C.: American Council on Education, 1959).

III

Discipline and Method

A college professor is a person devoted to a discipline. The word "discipline" is related to "disciple," though today both words have unfortunately lost much of their early connotation. Yet always a worthy discipline is demanding and severe in its requirements, and only the one who dedicates himself to it will ever become a leader.

There is a popular, half-sentimental question often heard today which demonstrates how prone educators are to indulge in oversimplification. It is this: Is it more important to teach *students* or to teach *subject matter*? In its worst form the question appears to suggest that the discipline is of minor importance. So prevalent an attitude doubtless led Professor Woodbridge some years ago to warn: "Respect for persons is what the old education neglected. It would be a pity, would it not, if the new should neglect respect for learning?" Unless there is great respect for the discipline one professes, there can be no possibility of adequate teaching.

Rationalization of the Discipline

Every teacher needs to be increasingly aware of the possibilities in his discipline both for his students and for himself. If the teacher is not aware of these values, he has a big job of homework to do. Any discipline which belongs in a college curriculum embodies values of many kinds. It is important to be conscious of them, and to help students to comprehend them.

Every teacher ought to be able to state his purposes in teaching every course on his schedule. One should never assume that because a course is in the curriculum the students understand its merits. Some courses are no more than hurdles in the minds of students.

Numerous studies of the objectives of college teachers have been made. Reports of these investigations often suggest a single conclusion: Many teachers are trying to get as much history, or English, or chemistry "into the heads" of their students as possible. Teaching is construed mainly as a pouring-in process. Some teachers appear even outraged when they are asked about their course objectives.

It is hardly an exaggeration to say that not a single question of importance can be intelligently answered regarding any course until its aims have been clarified. Only in terms of objectives can the content of the course be determined, and only in terms of objectives can appropriate method be decided upon. Often a teacher is forced into the lecture method because his class is large, yet even here specific objectives will require conscious adjustments in presentation.

Evaluation also is more or less meaningless except in terms of aim. A teacher must have some yardstick against which to measure his progress. Therefore, the first responsibility of the teacher is the determination of his own objectives. Emerson wrote once of a minister friend of his who, the poet said, "aimed at nothing and always hit it exactly." The warning may be applied widely.

Aims Should Be Written Out Aims should be clearly enough rationalized to be stated in writing. When they cannot be put into words, they are likely to be incomplete and perhaps even self-contradictory.

Many teachers hold that statements of purpose are most effective when they are shared with students. If the student is conscious of course aims, his work will be improved to the extent that he keeps his eye upon what is being attempted. One very successful teacher has long followed the custom of preparing a statement of purpose and method, and presenting it to his class for study at first sessions. Often the students have illuminating revisions to suggest. There follows then a careful discussion of best ways of approaching the new course. Students are not, in such a context, thrown into a new discipline and forced to wade around for a time in sheer confusion.

At the last class session, the same teacher returns with the original statement of purpose. Discussion then centers upon how realistic the guidelines were, and what changes are indicated for another year. Such a process leads to continuing revision of aim, as well as readjustment in course content and method.

Types of Course Objectives In his pioneering book *College Teaching,* the late Paul Klapper suggests four types of course objectives. These are paraphrased here with full awareness that they do not exhaust the possibilities.

1. *The Informational Aim.* This is the objective which needs least explanation, since in many instances it is the only aim consciously held. *Information alone is easiest to evaluate.*

2. *The Disciplinary Aim.* By this aim is implied the achievement of power—*to reason about the material, to observe accurately, to discriminate between vital and unimportant detail, and to interpret.* Clearly, this aim may involve less attention to numbers of facts and more attention to problems. Just as the informational aim is likely to sacrifice mental development, the disciplinary aim may sacrifice facts.

3. *The Appreciative or Aesthetic Aim.* Some courses—perhaps all to a degree—aim primarily to develop in students *an appreciation of the arts of life.* When this aim is paramount, it is essential that students be brought directly into contact with the kind of work which will stimulate continuing eagerness to experience more and more of the art form. It is better to read poets than only to talk about them.

4. *The Development of Skill.* This aim does not, of course, apply only to technical subjects. A social science student ought to learn what the laboratory method is, and a student of the humanities should develop the power to find facts and use them to reach intelligent conclusions in the social sciences. A student should in all courses gain skill with language.[1]

Who shall decide which of these or other types of

[1] Paul Klapper, *College Teaching* (Tarrytown-on-Hudson, N. Y.: World Book Company, 1920), pp. 51 ff.

aims should be applied to any given course? Only the teacher. But unless he *decides,* he and his class may travel aimlessly.

The excitement and discipline which come from an effort to study purpose have been succinctly referred to in the following way:

> A stimulating experience for any teacher is to stop and ask himself why he teaches his subject. What is it for? What difference does he expect to result in his learners from having acquired it? How does it contribute to the growth of the learner? Many teachers confronted with this problem will say they teach it because it is good. This leads to the query, "Good for what? for whom? when? and why?"[2]

In brief, a teacher must have a task and a plan. Then he must have freedom to experiment. The task and the freedom can be supplied only by the institution. The plan and its constant readjustment are the first responsibilities of the teacher.

Method That method cannot be decided except in terms of basic aims is graphically illustrated by Paul Klapper in the book noted earlier:

> A professor of English literature boasted of the thoroughness with which he teaches *Hamlet.* "Every word of value and every change in the form of versification are marked; every allusion is taken up, every peculiar grammatical construction is brought to the attention of the class." Here we have (an illustration) of an erroneous

[2] Earl Clarence Kelley, *Education for What Is Real* (New York: Harper & Brothers, 1947).

> conception of thoroughness which gives it an extensive meaning and regards it as the accumulation of a mass of data.

The example indicates far more than a mere misconception of the idea of thoroughness. It shows equally a conscious or unconscious teaching purpose which neglects entirely many of the primary values of literature. It is highly possible that students who have labored carefully at such detail will not be constrained later to read Shakespeare by choice.

Should not all college courses be planned to help students to express themselves more accurately and more vigorously in their own tongue? This is one question that every teacher must face. It is commonplace knowledge that too few students are able to use the English language effectively. Frequently, therefore, the burden of teaching this basic skill is assigned to the department of English. Yet English teachers know all too well that unless students are required in all courses to develop their powers of expression, efforts of single departments are doomed to extremely limited success. Furthermore, it may be asked whether the student can handle any discipline adequately if he is unable to frame its concepts in his own words. The problem is again one of conscious aim.

It is possible to attempt so much in reaching the informational aim of the course that the major concepts which the facts produce are neglected or avoided. To be as up to date as possible in one's facts is essential; yet from the point of view of a growing student, the concepts to which the facts lead are of even greater value. The late American poet Edna St. Vincent Millay symbolized the point negatively, but still with much power:

> Upon this gifted age, in its dark hour,
> Falls from the sky a meteoric shower
> Of facts . . . they lie unquestioned, uncombined.
> Wisdom enough to leech us of our ill
> Is daily spun; but there exists no loom
> To weave it into fabric.[3]

There is no substitute, in the classroom or out, for sincere efforts at interpretation. Nor is there any excitement to be compared with that of seeing an important relationship for the first time.

Talk, Talk, Talk There has been much discussion of the values of the lecture method as opposed to other instructional techniques. Socrates, who used mainly a different approach, sharply criticized the Sophists for their lecturing. Criticism continues to this day. Yet lecturing is still the most common form of instruction in American colleges.

Beginning teachers are likely to use the method because they have had most of their experience with it. Moreover, the graduate school from which they have come has supplied them with a set of lecture notes which gets them started in their new endeavor. It will not be long, parenthetically, before the alert teacher discovers that the graduate-school notes which once

---

[3] Edna St. Vincent Millay, *Huntsman, What Quarry?* Harper & Brothers, New York, copyright © 1939. Used by permission of Norma Millay Ellis.

seemed so attractive to him are not necessarily useful to his own students. When the teacher arrives at this point, he is ready for a major advance in his work.

Professor Max Marshall in *Two Sides to a Teacher's Desk* estimates that at 200 words a minute, an instructor can deliver 10,000 words in a class period. In a course of thirty lectures, this means 300,000 words, or the equivalent of four novels. Dr. Marshall admits to having discovered once with dismay that he had uttered more words in his lectures for a single course than were contained in an excellent textbook which had few adoptions because it was "too long." [4]

The pros and cons of lecturing have been stated again and again, yet perhaps nowhere more effectively than by Sir Walter Moberly in *The Crisis in the University:*

The Lecture Method—Pro

1. It is less impersonal than a book—*nothing can replace the stimulus of a great teacher.*
2. It brings a man face to face with many students.
3. The best part is not what is said, but an attitude, a portion of the lecturer's faith which is passed on.

The Lecture Method—Con

1. It is a form of mass production, impersonal. . . .
2. It does not exercise the mind of the student, whose part is only to be a passive recipient. The student is writing for dear life, and becomes a recording machine.
3. It is incredibly wasteful of time. . . . Better to publish the lectures and circulate them.
4. It is positively harmful in that students come to think the lectures will supply all they need.

[4] Max S. Marshall, *Two Sides to a Teacher's Desk* (New York: The Macmillan Co., 1951), p. 23.

5. A large proportion of lectures are bad.

A student should not be taught more than he can think about. To profit from most lectures a student needs time to go over his notes carefully, to look up the references and to read at least some of the books mentioned. That is, he needs to spend a lot of time on them, other than in simply memorizing them, and in practice the time is seldom available.[5]

The point at issue in all this is again one of objective. Obviously matters of fact are more intelligently established by lecture or the student's reading than by discussion. There are other objectives, however, which may be achieved only by other methods, or by supplementation of lectures.

Much study has gone into nonlecture methods of teaching, and excellent visual aids are now available to make new approaches possible. Nevertheless in a study of the discussion method at the University of Chicago, instructors were surprised to discover that in recorded class sessions they had themselves done most of the talking. The recent book *Accent on Teaching*,[6] in which this experiment is reported, is one of the most helpful for the new teacher.

Evaluation of Teaching Every time a teacher gives an examination, he is evaluating not only his students, and the tone and quality of his institution, but also his own teaching. The criteria for good evaluation, accord-

[5] Sir Walter Moberly, *The Crisis in the University* (London: S. C. M. Press, 1949), pp. 19 ff.

[6] Sidney J. French, ed., *Accent on Teaching* (New York: Harper & Brothers, 1954), p. 23.

ing to C. Robert Pace of Syracuse University, are simply stated as follows:

1. How clear were the goals?
2. How complete, relevant, and scientifically valid were the means of obtaining and interpreting evidence?
3. What happened as a result of the evaluation?

Of these suggestions, the third is in some respects the most commonly neglected. Unless evaluation helps the teacher to improve either his goals, making them more comprehensive or more nearly achievable, or his methods, it has largely failed of its purpose. If there is no effort at evaluation, advance is only accidental.

Scholarship and Research It has been suggested earlier that if a teacher is to grow in his discipline he will want to plan his future with greatest care. Since teaching is the major function of the typical undergraduate institution, the temptation is always present to assume that good teaching and scholarship are somehow unrelated. They are, on the contrary, most closely related, just as are writing and teaching. William H. Cowley in *Toward Better College Teaching* proposes a distinction between research and scholarship which may prove helpful. Dr. Cowley suggests that the term *research* be applied to primary information and its understanding, but that *scholarship* be used to refer to the process by which primary information is made a part of the larger body of knowledge in any area.

Teaching apparently depends more upon the second process than the first. Thus the one who masters the results of scholarship, and uses them in the developing concepts he is teaching, is performing an essential service. By this definition scholarship at its best produces a fresh and creative synthesis of facts already at hand. There is hardly a challenge likely to stimulate more intellectual activity among college teachers than the desire to develop new insights upon old yet fundamental problems.

Teaching Requires Planning Teaching is an art, and as such requires careful planning. Gilbert Highet in *The Art of Teaching* has described vividly the care with which William Lyon Phelps, considered by some the best teacher of his day, prepared for his first course of lectures:

> He distributed guide sheets which (a) gave full outlines of every lecture, (b) advised books to be read concurrently, and (c) invited written or spoken questions.[7]

This is, of course, an illustration of only one man's approach to his profession. Yet it suggests sharply the careful preparation which contributed to Phelps's success. At times teachers fail because they expect too little in results, and therefore plan inadequately.

While many teachers plan carefully for their day-to-day work, they fail in long-range planning. Thus their courses lack symmetry and completeness. Who indeed has not been disappointed by a graduate course which began on a high level, gradually drifted off into de-

[7] Gilbert Highet, *The Art of Teaching* (New York: Alfred A. Knopf, Inc., 1950).

tailed trivia, and at long last failed to reach the point at which any important conclusions or insights could be achieved?

The Syllabus—Pro and Con There is a long-standing debate in educational circles about the value of the syllabus. Some say that the syllabus tends to crystallize a course, and thus limits its flexibility. Others insist that unless the instructor has some clear view of the progress of his course, it is likely to be wasteful in time, and more important, in lack of focus. Perhaps there is reason to both positions, yet the greater danger is always this: that the course will be without discernible direction or without any vital link to other courses. A syllabus can be a map without becoming a rigid schedule. The syllabus should be adjustable from day to day, but some plan is essential for the teacher, even though students never see it.

One clear evidence of the growth of the faculty member is the development of his syllabi from year to year. This practice might well be used as one test of his readiness for advancement. *In any event, is it not possible to say that if the teacher does not know where the course is going, the students will not?*

Teaching and Writing Should the emphasis be placed on teaching or writing? This question is often debated as though there were a real clash between the two. Actually the problem is not *either* teaching *or* writing. The vital teacher will do both, normally and naturally.

Teachers in small colleges especially are wont to complain of such heavy loads that they have no time for writing. There is often substance to the contention, and in these cases relief must be earnestly sought. In most instances, however, time for writing can be found. The fact is that when continued study and the writing which it produces are not a part of the teacher's discipline, he has not properly appraised his profession.

Much so-called scholarly writing is trivial and even foolish. The ritualistic production of so many pages per year in order to publish or perish is of itself relatively valueless. But when writing is closely linked to teaching, the result is certain to be an increase in vitality. There is also no way to avoid the evaluation of a teacher at least in part by the kind and quality of his writing. Administrators and faculty members are justified in considering this as one important requirement for advancement.

As the debate between writing and teaching has continued, so the argument between specialization and general understanding has a long history. A teacher must, obviously, specialize in something, but his specialty ought to be in an area of actual relevance to the purposes of the liberal arts college, if this is to be his place of work.

As he gains power in his discipline, the teacher's own general education must continue so that the relationship of his specialty to the liberal arts enterprise will be constantly and increasingly apparent. When this is not done, the possibilities of the liberal arts are being surrendered by assumed friends.

This means that a teacher must be a constant and

wide reader—within and without his major field. It is essential that he establish early for himself a general plan of reading. Each teacher should from time to time re-examine his reading practices, and thus reappraise his own intellectual development. It has been wisely noted that the single way to make a course relevant is to keep the teacher relevant.

Every college community offers numerous opportunities for the mutual enrichment of its members. Concerts, lectures, discussion groups, athletic events—all these and many others are available to the faculty member. It is disheartening to observe, nevertheless, how often important campus lectureships are attended only by those in the sponsoring discipline. It is even more disturbing at times to see how little use is made of the college library by those who are primarily responsible for making it a source of vital growth for students.

The Problem of Routine A noted teacher once remarked that teaching must be done "on time." By this he meant that the class schedule can prove to be a tyrant. The point suggests some of the dangers inherent in formal teaching. Routine can be very helpful if it is constantly evaluated and adjusted to educational objectives. Otherwise the routine becomes a rut, mechanically followed and deadly. Here is one of the major problems of the teaching profession.

When the teacher retreats to his routine, he is unfortunately sure to find that he can "get by," just as do his students, with little creative work. Laziness, it has been said, is our most pleasant vice. To avoid this and other dangers, the teacher must revise his courses regularly and continue to evaluate his methods and effectiveness. Too many veteran teachers fail to do anything at all about either revision or evaluation.

In concluding this chapter, perhaps we need to be reminded again of the words of Paul H. Buck of Harvard regarding the teaching profession: "We are part of a great continuity." Quite so!

IV

Teacher and Student

WHEN all has been said and done, a true college exists to bring together student and teacher in a community of common purpose. This purpose is learning and teaching. A university might exist without students, but not a college. *The single fundamental function of a college administration is, therefore, to help develop the best possible environment in which learning and teaching can take place.* Obviously this includes more than the classroom, yet classroom and library are the key features in the college community.

So Cardinal Newman wrote with reason:

> I say then, that the personal influence of the teacher is able in some sort to dispense with an academical system, but that system cannot in any way dispense with personal influence. . . . An academical system without the personal influence of teachers upon pupils, is an Arctic winter; it will create an ice-bound, petrified, cast-iron University, and nothing else.

Among the few best gifts of life are those teachers whose influence has made a difference in students. Isaac Newton, in explaining his scientific achievements, once testified: "I stood on the shoulders of giants." Many people can speak in similar terms of their teachers. It is in the classroom that the miracle of education most frequently begins.

A favorite indoor sport on most campuses is to deplore the lack of quality and academic interest in the student body. There can be no doubt that much of the criticism is justified. It has always been so. No student body is ideal from the point of view of the teacher, and admissions policies must receive continuing study. Poorly motivated and incompetent students do not make for a strong college. Yet a teacher must begin with the students he has. A strange paradox should be noted at this point. It is this: Even as teachers complain of student ability and preparation, they tend to grade them generously. How high grades fit low-quality students it would be difficult to say.

The College and the Secondary School

Today it is accepted practice for colleges to blame the high schools for the poor preparation of the student. However, since the liberal arts colleges train a large proportion of secondary schoolteachers, the colleges have a burden of criticism to bear also. Therefore, the training of teachers ought never to be delegated to departments of education alone.

It is unfortunate that the average college teacher knows so little about the public schools of his community, and feels small responsibility for them beyond assessing blame. Dr. Charles H. Wilson, superintendent of schools in Highland Park, Illinois, writes that liberal arts professors have taken almost no active interest in the schools of his community. He says:

> Since I started to teach twenty years ago, I have not once seen a liberal arts professor in a school except by

> invitation. I have not known one liberal arts professor to attend a superintendents' round table or teachers' meeting. . . . How many times do you suppose the history and English professors of Northwestern University or Lake Forest College, both of which are within a few minutes' drive, have stopped in my office, or stopped by to visit a former teacher, in the past six years? Not one.[1]

It may be that there is an important implication in these words which all teachers should heed.

As a starter, subject-matter professors ought to observe the student teachers they have helped to prepare. Such a practice would represent a natural link between school and college.

What Can Be Done? Some liberal arts colleges have labored to improve understanding between high-school and college teachers. One plan is to bring teachers in a given discipline to the campus for a day of study and discussion. One small college in the Midwest recently invited English teachers to a carefully planned session on new views of Shakespeare. The intellectual results were far more exciting than anticipated, but mutual understanding was the chief gain.

Many colleges now follow their teaching alumni through correspondence and by other methods. These colleges are thus aware of information which not only reflects the college's work but also influences its future programs.

Since an important problem confronting every college is the orientation of new students, the high school-

[1] Charles H. Wilson, *A Teacher Is a Person* (New York: Holt, Rinehart & Winston, Inc., 1956), pp. 112, 113.

college articulation conference has become increasingly common. One approach is to invite to the campus principals or counselors from nearby high schools which enroll substantial numbers of students in the college. During the morning the visitors interview individually students from their schools who are concluding their first college year. This is an important time in the student's life. After luncheon with college administration and department heads, there is an informal but frank discussion of what the interviewers have learned. The results are nearly always positive. They indicate changes of approach which the college may wish to consider. They show points at which the high-school program should be rethought.

Important by-products of such plans are that high-school and college people meet together to consider serious mutual problems. Each group comes to a better understanding of the difficulties the other confronts. Henceforth there is likely to be much less antagonism and less irresponsible criticism. The device has indirect public relations values of first importance, too.

How Strong Are College Students? More people are attending college than ever before. Whereas in 1900 only about 4 per cent of college-age students entered colleges or universities, by 1956 more than 20 per cent were in institutions of higher education, and in California more than 50 per cent. By 1970 there may be more than 4,000,000 students in colleges and universities. The number may, in fact, reach 5,500,000 by 1970 if the present annual increase in percentage of those attending college is maintained. Obviously, fewer selective factors are operating to keep students out of college.

The results are apparent. Students generally have appeared poorly grounded in the language arts, in mathematics and the sciences, and in some areas of the social studies. There is much evidence, however, that high-school work is steadily gaining strength.

Today's students are on the whole healthier, happier, and perhaps better balanced than former groups. They are more nearly a cross section of American life than ever before. They come from homes representing a wider social base and more occupations. Today three fourths of American college students come from these occupational groups: proprietary, agricultural, professional, and managerial; but more than before come from skilled and unskilled labor.[2]

The geographical pattern of college attendance has altered little. In a recent United States Office of Education study, it is revealed that four out of five undergraduate students attend college in their home states, and most of the other fifth in adjacent states. Unfortunately perhaps, most students go home over week ends, making the full benefits of traditional residential study more difficult to achieve.

The mean intelligence of American students entering liberal arts colleges has been estimated at 115 IQ, a level which would be exceeded by fewer than 20 per cent of the total population. An IQ of 110 has long been held as a minimum necessary for successful liberal arts college work.

[2] *Encyclopedia of Educational Research* (New York: The Macmillan Co., Revised, 1950).

Why Do Students Enter College? Many studies have been made to determine why students enter college. Over the years, major reasons given by students have been the following in the order given: (1) vocational preparation, (2) cultural improvement, (3) interest in certain studies, (4) prestige, (5) parents' wishes. It is clear that as in former years, students go to college for utilitarian, cultural, and other reasons. *Most teachers who can remember their own student days will recognize that these were their purposes too.* There is actually little point in deploring the aims of college students. The college can, however, demonstrate in many ways the full opportunities of campus life.

Every teacher will profit from reading the pamphlet *They Come for the Best of Reasons.*[3] This brief but positive treatment will help to eliminate some of the foolish oversimplifications we are prone to make about students.

The more a teacher knows about his students, the more effective he is likely to be with them. Much information is available on every campus. It is particularly important to know which students are unusually promising, and which will require special attention. At the same time, no teacher dare assume from previous records that a student cannot improve. Students, like teachers, are not to be imprisoned by the past.

What Students Look for in Teachers Many lists have been made of desirable qualities in

[3] Max W. Wise, *They Come for the Best of Reasons* (Washington, D. C.: American Council on Education, 1958).

teachers, some by professional educators as a result of observation and study, some from student polls (which many teachers refuse to take seriously), and others by teachers themselves. Doubtless there is some potential value in almost all such studies.

In 1947 Brooklyn College examined the students' view of what was wanted in teaching. The resulting report, entitled *The Student Looks at His Teacher* (1950), was based mainly upon a careful use of questionnaires. Parenthetically, two out of every three Brooklyn College teachers voted in favor of repeating the survey.

What did the students look for in their teachers? The following statements paraphrase major Brooklyn College conclusions:

1. Students want a high level of scholarly competence.
2. Students especially value teaching which stimulates individual thought.
3. Students look for teachers with the ability to explain their disciplines and to organize their work interestingly and effectively.
4. Students place value upon the teacher's enthusiasm for his subject.
5. Students appreciate teachers who give fair examinations.[4]

It is useful to add that in general younger instructors were rated higher than older ones on the above list except in knowledge of subject matter.

[4] John W. Riley, *et al.*, *The Student Looks at His Teacher* (New Brunswick, N. J.: Rutgers University Press, 1950).

The Able Teacher In a study made by professional educators assigned the task of examining the problem of preparation for medical education in the liberal arts colleges of the United States, the authors offer the following as essential characteristics of teachers:

1. Belief in his subject and continual intellectual and spiritual nourishment from significant study and research.
2. Power to apprehend significance, and to go beyond mere facts to interpretations and conclusions of real human import.
3. Love of young people, and an eagerness to share his ongoing search with them. The teacher must be eager to strengthen (the students') faith in themselves, and in the possibility of a world of diminishing fear and increasing hope. He must understand the psychology of adolescence and youth.
4. Respect for his craft as a teacher, and a determination to perfect himself more and more in the skills of scholarship and instruction.
5. A sense of responsibility to the institution with which he is associated.
6. Community-mindedness.[5]

It is essential, according to this report, that a "teacher take inventory of himself from time to time, not merely with respect to his professional skills, important as these are, but psychologically, philosophically, and religiously as well." The check list suggested in an earlier chapter can serve as such an inventory.

---

[5] Aura E. Severinghaus, *et al.*, *Preparation for Medical Education in the Liberal Arts College* (New York: McGraw-Hill Book Co., Inc., 1953).

The Poor Teacher Paradoxically perhaps, it appears easier to characterize poor teaching than good. Many lists of undesirable teaching practices have been promulgated, some based on student judgments, others on professional studies. Among the best known of the professional lists is the following by Louella Cole:

1. *Scholarship*
   A. The poor teacher does not know his subject matter and is often out of date.
   B. He does not continue to work and study in his field.
   C. He is often interested primarily in either research or writing, and not in teaching.
2. *Handling of class*
   A. He does not control his class; he assigns reading and books that are not in the library; he does not allow time enough for the work.
   B. He does not use an outline or syllabus; he jumps from one thing to another in an illogical fashion.
   C. He is vague and indecisive in class; he rambles; he has no discernible objective; he bluffs and stalls.
   D. He uses the same methods day after day; he depends almost wholly upon the textbook, practically paralleling it in class; he is so dependent upon his notes he cannot look at the students while he talks. He sometimes reads his lectures.
   E. He has no clear standard of work.
   F. He often makes no assignment; when he does, he assigns only pages in text.
   G. He makes no effort to connect what goes on in class with anything outside; he repeats the examples given in the text and rarely has supplementary materials of his own.
   H. His tests are poorly made and unfair; he sometimes does not pass back papers; when he does return them, he delays for several days; he gives them no

help in reviewing; his grading is inaccurate and careless.

I. He does not allow his students to talk much, and does not permit them to disagree with him.

J. He talks over his students' heads; he is technical.

K. He makes no evident effort to individualize his work.

L. He uses poor English; he has numerous annoying mannerisms.

3. *Personality*

A. He is lazy, conceited, impatient, indifferent.

B. He is sarcastic, prejudiced, dogmatic, intolerant; he shows marked favoritism.

C. He is dull.

D. He will not admit errors or shortcomings.

E. He has either no humor or unkind humor.

F. He is untidy and unsystematic.[6]

It would be difficult to create a more searching list of potential weaknesses than this. In any case, enough has already been written to indicate that a teacher succeeds or fails *with students*. In pure research, this is not so. In the liberal arts college, however, success must be measured by what is done for and with students.

Putting the Burden Upon the Student

Nothing is more important, or more difficult, than getting the student personally involved in his own education. Woodrow Wilson is credited with having once said: "You cannot educate a man. He must do that for himself." Yet it often takes a good teacher even to

[6] Louella Cole, *The Background of College Teaching* (New York: Farrar and Rinehart, 1940), pp. 561-562.

bring the student to the place of educating himself.

The same thing has been said in another way by Huston Smith:

> If the liberal arts college's accomplishments are restricted to what it can inject into students in from two to four years, its possibilities are not very exciting. But if, on the other hand, it can change students from barges that must be towed into self-propelling ships, its effects will be carried on down the years. Stated in academic terms, the aim of education is to change pupils into students.[7]

This is, therefore, the core of the teacher's assignment. Students must be increasingly required to act as maturing, responsible individuals. Teachers should not do for students what students ought to do for themselves. Those who have no intention of applying themselves, or no ability to grasp the significance of the opportunity before them, should be encouraged to leave the campus. As enrollments increase in the years immediately ahead, the colleges can upgrade the entire educational structure of the nation by being both more stimulating and more demanding.

Among many wholesome signs of the present are new efforts to develop independent study programs and to stimulate more fully the brightest student. Required reading is *The Independent Study Program in the United States.*[8] In this book is suggested some of the range of current efforts in the field, but especially helpful is the analysis of the College of Wooster

---

[7] Huston Smith, *The Purposes of Higher Education* (New York: Harper & Brothers, 1955).

[8] Robert H. Bonthius, *et al.*, *The Independent Study Program in the United States* (New York: Columbia University Press, 1957).

(Ohio) program which *requires* independent study of all graduates.

Another helpful instrument is *The Superior Student,* a newsletter published monthly during the school year by the Inter-University Committee on the Superior Student. This is sent free to interested persons on request.[9]

The Strongest and the Weakest A teacher is often confronted with a wide range of capacity and interest in his classes. Shall he pitch his work at the level of the best, the average, or the poorest?

Several considerations are important. From the strongest are likely to come most of those who will qualify as leaders of the future. The teacher and the college have a special responsibility for these, and ways must be found to excite and encourage them. Special assignments and more independent work are indicated. Every experienced teacher has found in the development of some of the best students his greatest satisfaction and reward.

One danger in approaching the slower members of a class is that the teacher will condemn them out of hand. Some students are slow starters who have never before been fully challenged. They have never been truly motivated. There are self-helps in every field which the earnest student can employ to bring himself up to necessary levels. Yet the most promising student must not be held back, nor allowed to coast, while the

[9] *The Superior Student,* Inter-University Committee on the Superior Student, 112 Hellems, University of Colorado, Boulder, Colorado.

slower one catches up. A famed language teacher once characterized the American tendency to aim instruction at the poorest students in these words: "Blessed is he in America who is born a moron." There is more than a touch of truth in the jest.

As to the "average" student, he too must be made to reach. He ought never to be castigated for being average. But neither should he be allowed to settle for mediocrity if he can reach higher. The disciples of Jesus were evidently "average" men, but they moved and shook the world.

More Than Classrooms A college is more than a group of teachers in classrooms, and students are educated twenty-four hours a day. The devoted teacher will, therefore, accept his share of the guidance function of the college. In the counseling sessions the teacher will have opportunities to share personally his own insights with his students. Counseling is never to be taken lightly. Many major victories have been won during a quiet talk.

Friendship between student and teacher is a value which can never be overestimated. Teachers are often surprised by the eagerness of students to meet them as friends. Dr. D. Elton Trueblood has this to say about the matter: "One of the major tragedies in modern college experience is the lack of friendship between students and teacher. It is our open scandal. I have visited many colleges where there is a frank recognition that the community is broken at this vital point." [10]

[10] D. Elton Trueblood, "The Idea of a College," *Association of American Colleges Bulletin,* March, 1950, p. 35.

Dr. Trueblood holds that a major reason for this "break" in the community is that the same person is both teacher and judge. He urges that examinations be given by outsiders, and that student and teacher regard themselves as comrades in a great task.

Kermit Eby has summarized a point of view in the following way:

> As I have said before, if you don't love 'em, you can't teach 'em. Love involves the heart as well as the mind, and we are in this association not teachers and pupils, but seekers who aspire to the goodly fellowship out of which all that is good in history springs. . . . Jesus, Buddha, Confucius, Socrates . . . these were the great teachers who struck a spark that lit the world. I only ask that my spark, though it be a little one, will suffice.[11]

This suggestion leads directly to a consideration of the college community.

[11] Kermit Eby, "A Man Named Andrew," *The Christian Century*, November 17, 1954.

V

The College a Community

"Men work together," I told him from the heart,
"Whether they work together or apart." [1]

A vital college is far more than an aggregate of individuals, each going his own way. To produce full results, a college must be distinguished by a community spirit, with a life and ethos of its own. The function of this community is not only, as educators are often tempted to say, to prepare students for life, but also to make possible at once an intensity of living which is likely never again to be duplicated in the experience of its members.

Intellectual zest is at the heart of the community spirit, but the intellectual life must be characterized also by creativeness, mutuality of concern, and a hopefulness regarding the future. The academic community is dedicated to the belief that people can be changed as they grow in knowledge and wisdom.

The Basic Groups There are at least three discrete units represented on any campus, each with its own peculiar interests and responsibilities. These groups are: (1) the student body, (2) the faculty, (3) the administrative staff and board of trustees.

Splits within these groups develop naturally and in-

[1] Robert Frost, "The Tuft of Flowers."

evitably. The student body breaks up into fraternities and sororities, as well as into other units. The faculty readily divides into powerful, and at times self-seeking, departments. The administrative staff has its own possibilities of cleavage.

More than occasionally the alumni and other constituencies create major problems, and represent still other group interests. There are thus times when a campus represents anything but a unified community, acting rather like the character of whom H. G. Wells said: "She was not so much a human being as a civil war." The possibilities of the true campus community have forced some educators to conclude that the larger the institution, the more difficult to achieve the best college life.

A Sense of Purpose A true educational community must be characterized by common purposes. This does not assume even for a moment that diversity is not desirable on the campus. It is the diversity among highly trained and gifted men and women that makes a campus stimulating and exciting. When individual opinion is lacking, only dullness results. Yet amid diversity of gift and point of view there must be common goals, and the unity which comes from intelligent compromise and adjustment. When everyone goes his own way, the potential values of community spirit are lost. The result is likely to be sheer chaos. This danger has been expressed by Robert Hutchins in his *Education for Freedom:*

> A community implies that people are working together, and people cannot work together unless they have common principles and purposes. If half a crew of men are tearing down a house as the other half are building it, we do not say they are working together. If half a group of people are engaged in robbing, cheating, oppressing, and killing the other half, we should not say the group is a community. Common principles and purposes create a community; justice, by which we mean a fair allocation of functions, rewards, and punishments, in terms of the rights of man and the principles and purposes of the community, holds it together.[2]

Each of the three fundamental campus groups has its own unique function and responsibility. It is primarily for the students that a college exists. The universities may have functions other than teaching, but not the college. Students are both teachers and learners, but their primary task is learning. The teaching staff represents the hope that the college will be an instrument of power. Teachers must by definition be learners if they would teach well. Yet teaching is the prime service of the faculty member.

The administrative staff is assigned the task of making teaching and learning possible, and of giving the process the best environment in which to proceed. When administrators forget this function, and see their work as an end in itself, their usefulness is lost. Since their responsibilities are tremendous, administrators should not be subjected to irresponsible attack by other units of the community, especially by a thoughtless faculty. Irresponsibility only aggravates difficulties.

[2] Robert M. Hutchins, *Education for Freedom* (Baton Rouge, La.: Louisiana State University Press, 1943).

Dr. Harry Emerson Fosdick once preached a powerful sermon whose title was: "Are We Part of the Problem or Part of the Answer?" It is a question every member of the academic community should at times put to himself.

Nurturing the Community In dealing with the academic community, it is always a temptation to give easy answers to difficult problems. Yet answers must be sought. What are the basic principles for high campus morale? What can the individual teacher do to bear his share of responsibility?

1. The first requirement in the building of a true academic community is a sense of mutual purpose.

It is possible, of course, to spend so much time examining institutional and individual aims as never actually to get to the job in hand. There is little value in any mere verbal juggling of statements of purpose. Yet it is clear that any community needs a point of agreement and emphasis. Education, *per se,* is not necessarily beneficial; but only that education which has reason and purpose.

It is, therefore, the institutions with traditions of excellence which become instruments of educational power, those which know what they are about and hold firmly and as a group to college goals. These aims are, however, more than verbal exercises. They are rallying points which may prove disciplinary upon college activities. They cannot be static, but they must be understood and vitally accepted.

The Image of the College It has long been understood that the image people have of themselves has great influence upon their behavior. Likewise, the image of the college in the minds of faculty and staff will determine to a great degree what the college becomes.

Often new administrators are forced to struggle with images in the faculty and public mind which hamper progress. In such cases a new image is needed. What is the intellectual tone of the campus to be? What sort of educational product should the college strive for? What admission standards are required to reach the goals desired? What are the distinguishing functions of the college? These and a host of similar questions bristle up as a college labors to define its aims.

Thinking Otherwise After institutional goals are once agreed upon, the alternatives for the faculty member who does not approve are basically two. He can refuse to go along and in subtle or obvious ways undermine the community. Or he can accept the will of the majority and labor to determine whether the avowed purposes are possible of achievement. He has a right, always, to be part of the loyal minority which feels obligated to effect changes, and to speak out in faculty meetings and committees. When, however, there is public disagreement, before students, for example, the community spirit is jeopardized.

Thus when a college sets certain directions, other directions are eliminated in the process. Pet courses of individual teachers may at times be inappropriate to the established goals, or may prove too expensive. Revised methods of instruction are required if certain aims are to be achieved. Here, as in all community living, an individual can go his own way, insisting always upon his personal desires, but only at the expense of the institution's spirit.

Thoughtful commitment to an educational ideal and plan helps to produce a true community. When this commitment is not possible, the least that should be expected of a faculty member is that he will accept the decision of the majority, and not intentionally undermine the unity of the college.

Fellowship Is More Than a Word Simeon Stylites, late celebrated commentator of *The Christian Century,* has suggested whimsically the importance of the need for fellowship in a common concern:

> Fellowship that is more than a nice word is always built around some kind of work, among people who are doing a job. Whenever people say, "Go to now, let's have fellowship, just in itself," the result is a sorry fizzle. Who knows, perhaps there might be more fellowship in the churches of the sort that still pulses in the pages of the New Testament, if there were more people working on a job.[3]

When an important common job has been accepted by the group, the first requirement of a true community has been met. What is more, there will emerge

---

[3] Simeon Stylites, *The Christian Century,* July 29, 1953. Copyright, 1953, Christian Century Foundation. Reprinted by permission.

a sense of fellowship and unity without which work together is tasteless.

The faculty member will confront constant opportunities to help in the creation of a vital academic community. His teaching is his major point of contact. How does he link his work to the basic purposes of the college? Does he know how to relate his teaching to that of his colleagues, thus eliminating the obvious dangers of overdepartmentalism? Does he help students to share the aims of the college community? Does he take seriously his part of the guidance burden of the college? Is he positive of his respect for the college in his campus as well as his public appearances?

2. A second requirement in the building of an academic community is sharing in major college decisions.

It may appear at first glance that this principle applies primarily to administrative officers. That participation in decision-making depends upon the extent to which such is invited or permitted is of course clear. A thoughtless, insensitive administration can deny the principle by its actions.

Yet faculty members also have important responsibilities here. For example, it is the teacher who has closest contact with the student. Does the teacher regard his students as more than passive participants in the educational enterprise? Does he welcome student suggestions in the courses he teaches? Some teachers are occasionally more autocratic in their relationships to students than administrative officers at their worst could be to faculty members.

The efforts of a college administration for gaining consensus vary widely from place to place. Most colleges, however, provide for faculty committees to deal more or less directly with college policies. Often faculty committees on a given campus are multiplied beyond usefulness. Committee work should be cut to the minimum essentials. At times committees deal with routine matters which should be left to administrative officers. Nevertheless, there is possibility for actual participation in important decision-making in the committee structure of the college.

Faculty Meetings The faculty meeting offers a formal opportunity for exchange of ideas regarding the direction of the college. These meetings may, like the work of committees, deal mainly with the routine and trivial. Each teacher must bear his share of the responsibility for the morale and power of faculty meetings.

The conscientious participation of the individual teacher in deciding basic issues affecting the college represents the community at its best. It is here that the good of the whole is at issue, but only responsible thoughtfulness can produce essential results.

Dean Esther Rauschenbush of Sarah Lawrence College has aptly summarized the point:

> I propose to describe faculty morale as the product of the commitment faculty members in a college are able to make to their college. I suggest that it is high in direct proportion to the amount of investment, the sense of possession or ownership the faculty have in the college itself. This sense of commitment is much more possible to achieve in a small college, I think, than in a large university.

> We know, indeed, that many people in large universities do have such feelings about their institution, and we know too, unfortunately, that life in some small colleges is made dreary by its absence. In a large university the feeling of commitment is more often a happy condition of the teachers' immediate surroundings than a part of the design of the institution itself; in a small college it is likely to be the consequence of intelligent planning for the whole institution.
>
> When I say "commitment" I do not mean blind and uncritical loyalty; nor inbreeding; nor living totally within the walls of the college. In fact, commitment is more likely to be felt by a professor who has an interested and interesting life outside the college as well as in it, and it is much more likely to result in good for the individual and the college as well.[4]

This attitude on the part of a college dean summarizes effectively the mutual responsibility of faculty and administration to understand and to share. Where there is less than this, the community is certain to suffer.

Individual and Corporate President Louis T. Benezet of Colorado College has stated the alternatives in this way:

> The college professor is a specialist who still must develop a high degree of corporate sense. Because his actions and attitudes so vitally affect his corporation, he needs to have a share in corporation policy. Yet because he is a nonadministrative specialist he must also have relative freedom from management routine. Teaching takes time. Properly done, an average teaching load, with all its attendant responsibilities to students, is enough to occupy the waking hours of everyone.[5]

[4] Esther Rauschenbush, Unpublished address, Danforth Summer Seminar, 1957.

[5] Louis T. Benezet, "How Many Cooks?" *President's Bulletin Board Reprint* (Nashville, Tenn.: Board of Education, The Methodist Church, 1956).

The "corporate sense" of which President Benezet writes will, of course, never develop where faculty members are held to be employees hired to do a specific but limited job. Teachers are *not* employees in the usual sense of the term. *They are members of a community in which functions are divided but goals shared.*

3. A third requirement in the building of an academic community is a conscious and continuing communication among its members.

Here again it is easy to assume that only administrative officers have anything important to communicate. Nothing could be further from the truth. It must be recognized, of course, that administration deals with many matters which affect faculty members in crucial ways—salaries, advancement in rank, new equipment, public relations, to mention only a few. In these matters an administration ought to find ways of keeping faculty members constantly "in on the know." As far as salaries and advancement are concerned, there should be carefully formulated principles available in writing. Sincere consultation on such matters should be the rule of the campus.

There are, however, many potential developments known to the administration which cannot be made public, or announced even to the faculty. Often premature announcement endangers the opportunity. In these instances the faculty should willingly accept the responsibility of administration and trustees for determining when information is to become public. The faculty often find themselves in a parallel role regarding student affairs.

Nevertheless, the college community should be a

place of continuing and friendly communication among its members—between faculty and students, between college departments, between departments and divisions, between administration and faculty. Channels of communication must be maintained in all directions.

Rights and Obligations Faculty members have more or less clearly defined rights and obligations. These should always be open for discussion. It is essential to bear in mind that obligations and rights are correlative, not independent. In a recent study Charles Dennison lists sixteen fundamental principles practiced by eight selected Eastern colleges of outstanding reputation. The principles, here paraphrased, merit continuing thought:

Faculty Rights and Obligations

1. Clear and mutually binding terms of appointment
2. Clear understanding of appointment duration and opportunities for promotion
3. Fair process of reappointment, promotions, and increments
4. Tenure
5. Advance notice of nonreappointment (*with corresponding obligation for advance faculty resignation notice*)
6. Due process on dismissals
7. Clear and consistent salary policy, with adequate consultation with those affected by it
8. Assistance in personal and family welfare
9. Stature and recognition in a profession dedicated to truth

10. Equal consideration regardless of personality and creed
11. Professional leaves of absence
12. Recognition of rights as well as institutional restraints in academic freedom
13. Regard for the rights and responsibilities of students
14. Rights and freedom within the department or division
15. Full participation in the over-all community role of college faculty
16. Access to the governing board of the institution[6]

Most governing boards and college administrations would endorse and accept these principles. Faculty members should understand that they involve major responsibilities on their part also.

The Letter and the Spirit Recently developed practices for improving relationships between the various campus groups show much promise. Among these are faculty handbooks, prepared usually by a joint faculty and administrative committee; faculty councils named to meet intermittently with administrative officers to discuss mutual concerns; faculty-student committees to treat informally matters which seem important; occasional coffee hours bringing together administrative and student officers. It is becoming common also to have an annual faculty-trustee dinner at which one

[6] Charles Dennison, *Faculty Rights and Obligations* (New York: Teachers College, Columbia University, 1955).

group may become more fully acquainted with the other.

Yet all planning and regulation are of little consequence unless there is an attitude of friendship on the campus. The letter of the law may kill; it is only the spirit which gives life. Thus in spite of the most carefully evolved regulations to assure fair treatment, community morale will be low where there is among members constant bickering and jealousy resulting from carelessness on the part of any group.

Academic Freedom High among the responsibilities of the faculty member is the proper understanding and practice of academic freedom. Academic freedom is assuredly not a right given to one profession in preference to another. It is basically a protection for society itself, allowing the teacher to express the truth as he discovers it. Of course a teacher may be mistaken, but error can never be identified and known for what it is if the freedom of sincere expression is lost. The whole problem has been succinctly noted in these words:

> With regard to some occupations, it is eminently in the interest of society that the men concerned speak their minds without fear of retribution. . . . The occupational work of the vast majority of people is largely independent of their thought and speech. . . . The professor's work *consists* of his thought and speech. . . . If some professors lose their positions for what they write or say, the effect on many other professors will be such that their usefulness to society will be gravely reduced.[7]

[7] Fritz Machlup, "On Some Misconceptions Concerning Academic Freedom," American Association of University Professors *Bulletin*, Winter, 1955.

Academic freedom is not a special privilege given to a single group, but it is the only method by which the teaching profession may make its full contribution to society. A nation may destroy this freedom, but in so doing it will also lose the self-criticism absolutely essential to its own liberty and vitality. There are no freedoms without commensurate responsibilities. Academic freedom is possible only when teachers are a highly responsible and thoughtful group, dedicated to the search for truth.

No teacher has the right to use his position irresponsibly. He must remember that he is an expert only in the field of his competence, and not in every area under the sun. He must remember particularly that he is working with a young and impressionable group who look to him for guidance in their inquiries. He is not dealing with intellectual equals. In a fundamental sense he can hardly speak on important issues of the day without to a degree representing the institution with which he is related. This calls, therefore, not for institutional limitations, but for a thoughtful sense of responsibility on the part of the teacher himself.

The statement of principles on academic freedom and responsibility adopted jointly by the American Association of University Professors and the Association of American Colleges ought to be studied and restudied by all those truly concerned about academic freedom.

Important sections of this statement follow:

> The teacher is entitled to full freedom in research and in the publication of the results, subject to the adequate

performance of his other academic duties; but research for pecuniary return should be based upon an understanding with the authorities of the institution. The teacher is entitled to freedom in the classroom in discussing his subject, but he should be careful not to introduce into his teaching controversial matter which has no relation to his subject. Limitations of academic freedom because of religious or other aims of the institution should be clearly stated in writing at the time of the appointment.

The college or university teacher is a citizen, a member of a learned profession, and an officer of an educational institution. When he speaks or writes as a citizen, he should be free from institutional censorship or discipline, but his special position in the community imposes special obligations. As a man of learning and an educational officer, he should remember that the public may judge his profession and his institution by his utterances. Hence he should at all times be accurate, should exercise appropriate restraint, should show respect for the opinions of others, and should make every effort to indicate that he is not an institutional spokesman.

In January, 1961, the Association of American Colleges adopted new standards recommended by its Commission of Academic Freedom and Tenure. The statement is so important that it is given here in full:

Mobility of faculty members among colleges and universities is rightly recognized as desirable in American higher education. Yet the departure of a faculty member always requires changes within his institution, and may entail major adjustments on the part of his colleagues, the administration, and students in his field. Ordinarily a temporary or permanent successor must be found and appointed to either his position or the position of a colleague who is promoted to replace him.

In a period of expansion of higher education, such as

that already existing and promising to be even more intensified as a pattern for the coming years, adjustments are required more frequently as the number of positions and of transfers among institutions increases. These become more difficult than at other times, especially in the higher academic ranks. Clear standards of practice in the recruitment and in the resignations of members of existing faculties should contribute to an orderly interchange of personnel that will be in the interest of all.

The standards set forth below are recommended to administration and faculties in the belief that they are sound and should be generally followed. They are predicated on the assumption that proper provision has been made by employing institutions for timely notice to probationary faculty members and those on term appointments, with respect to their subsequent status. In addition to observing applicable requirements for notice of termination to probationary faculty members, institutions should make provision for notice to all faculty members not later than March 15 of each year of their status the following fall, including rank and (unless unavoidable budget procedures beyond the institution forbid) prospective salary.

1. Negotiations looking to the possible appointment for the following fall of persons who are already faculty members of other institutions, in active service or on leave of absence and not on terminal appointment, should be begun and completed as early as possible in the academic year. It is desirable that, when feasible, the faculty member who has been approached with regard to another position inform the appropriate officers of his institution when such negotiations are in progress. The conclusion of a binding agreement for the faculty member to accept an appointment elsewhere should always be followed by prompt notice to his institution.

2. A faculty member should not resign in order to accept other employment as of the end of the academic year, later than May 15 or thirty days after receiving

notification of the terms of his continued employment the following year, whichever date occurs later. It is recognized, however, that this obligation will be in effect only if institutions generally observe the time factor set forth in the following paragraph for new offers. It is also recognized that emergencies will occur. In such an emergency the faculty member may ask the appropriate officials of his institution to waive this requirement; but he should conform to their decision.

3. To permit a faculty member to give due consideration and timely notice to his institution in the circumstances defined in paragraph 1 of these standards, an offer of appointment for the following fall at another institution should not be made after May 1. The offer should be a "firm" one, not subject to contingencies.

4. Institutions deprived of the services of faculty members too late in the academic year to permit their replacement by securing the members of other faculties in conformity to these standards, and institutions otherwise prevented from taking timely action to recruit from other faculties, should accept the necessity of making temporary arrangements or obtaining personnel from other sources, including new entrants to the academic profession and faculty personnel who have retired.

5. Except by agreement with his institution, a faculty member should not leave or be solicited to leave his position during an academic year for which he holds an appointment.

The Campus Climate

Obviously there are many forces outside the classroom influencing the American student. Some of these influences he brings with him; some rise out of the culture of which he is inevitably a part. Nevertheless, the campus climate or tone exerts, for good or ill, its own unmistakable pressure upon the student.

Important research is now going on to define the types of pressure exerted upon the student by the campus environment. Among these investigations may be noted the work of Nevitt Sanford at Vassar, of T. R. McConnell of the Center for the Study of Higher Education, California, and of C. Robert Pace of Syracuse University.

As an illustration only, it is useful to consider the "College Characteristics Index" devised by Dr. Pace and his associates. This is an instrument composed of 300 statements regarding college practices, designed to show the typical "press" of a given institution. The instrument has been exhaustively evaluated, and has been tried out in nearly 100 colleges and universities.

Typical statements from the above index include such as these:

> There is much interest in poetry, music, painting, sculpture, etc.
>
> The faculty encourage students to think about exciting and unusual careers.
>
> The school is outstanding in the emphasis it gives to scholarship and research.
>
> Class discussions are especially vigorous and intense.
>
> In many classes students have an assigned seat.
>
> Professors usually take attendance in class.

In general the Pace[8] studies indicate that college climates vary greatly, and that college practices actually determine what the climate is to be. Practices, not published statements of aim, define institutional objectives.

---

[8] For further information on this exciting approach, see C. Robert Pace and George G. Stern, "An Approach to the Measurement of Psychological Characteristics of College Environments," *Journal of Educational Psychology*, Vol. 49, No. 5, October, 1958, pp. 269-277.

For the individual teacher, two generalizations follow: First, his own practices help significantly to determine the campus tone. Second, only a conscious analysis of purposes and goals as compared to actual practice can bring us to see our own true influence.

The best possibilities of a college are inherent in two compelling factors. A college must be staffed by those who have individually dedicated themselves to the search for truth and to an intellectually responsible way of life. Again, a college can under appropriate conditions become a true community which wields a great influence over the future. This influence can be far beyond the aggregate of the abilities of those who compose it.

The Implications of Leadership One additional note is required in this brief treatment of the campus as a community. The problem concerns the exercise of leadership and authority.

It has been said earlier that the major function of a college administration is to help create an environment in which teaching and learning are expedited. The generalization is sound, but its application subject to much debate.

Final decisions on many critical campus matters cannot be made by committees. *Someone must finally be responsible.* In the American pattern of higher education, the college president is almost invariably the final authority. The president is in turn responsible directly to the governing board of the college. It is difficult to see how it could be otherwise.

College presidents, and to a lesser degree deans and business officers, must try to see the institution as a whole. Often they must make judgments which do not meet the approval of all segments of the faculty and student body. Presidents ought normally to be able, and willing, to give reasons for their actions on most important issues.

On the other hand, administrators have a right to expect that others will attempt also to see the whole issue, and that teachers will presume that administrators too want the best for their institution. Often with only the most fragmentary information, teachers take quite the opposite attitude. Likewise administrators must remember that teachers are at the heart of the educational process, and that if there is to be actual conquest on the campus, it will occur mainly because there has been a high-level encounter between a good teacher and a promising student.

Every college requires a sense of direction and stable leadership. Whether or not any real leadership can be exerted depends to a large degree upon the willingness *to listen*—on the part of both teachers and administrators.

VI

The Teacher and His Faith

EVERYTHING that has gone before must indicate that the teacher is the key factor in the development of an effective college community. It is the whole person, his whole approach to life, which determines the teacher's actual influence upon his students.

Every teacher's faith is at issue in his work. If he is teaching in a Christian college, he has even more profound responsibilities and opportunities.

In all sections of the country colleges and universities have been founded and fostered by those who believed strongly in a vital relationship between education and religion. To many this relationship has appeared to be mutually interdependent. They have held that education divorced from religion runs the risk of sterility, and that religion without education too easily becomes superstitious and anti-intellectual. Education *per se* leaves some important questions unanswered.

One of the Chinese characters in a recent book by Pearl Buck says of this matter: "To go to a college in America does not change a man's heart. It only gives him a new weapon, sharper than the old, to use against the people, if that be his heart." This is the same problem of which Harry Emerson Fosdick wrote so effectively in his recent autobiography. The statement appears in a chapter entitled significantly, "Ideas That Have Used Me."

> Today, however, education—indispensable and inexpressibly valuable though its contribution to human welfare has been—has become an aider and abettor of some of mankind's worst evils. To paraphrase a saying of George A. Buttrick, there is only one thing worse than a devil and that is an educated devil. That emphasis is a newcomer to America. We are not used to it. Education with us has had a halo over it. Ignorance is bad; education is good—that has been our simple formula. Our attention has been obsessed by the danger to democracy inherent in illiteracy, ignorance, stupidity. Of course they are dangerous to democracy. But when today one asks what we are most afraid of, what makes the shivers run up and down our spinal columns, it is not ignorant but educated devils, whether in Moscow or anywhere else—men with the know-how, the techniques of modern science in their grasp, the psychological skills for propaganda purposes, and all the rest, with the question rising: In heaven's name, what are they going to do with it?

Dr. Fosdick goes on logically to insist upon the necessity of an added requirement—the ethical—in education today:

> It is not primitive peoples who terrorize the world today, but educationally advanced peoples who make learning a road to power without bringing that power under ethical control. So I have lived into a generation where not science alone but education too "has created a world in which Christianity is an imperative." Facts without values, fragmentary specialities with no integrating philosophy of life as a whole, data with no ethical standards for their use, techniques either with no convictions about life's ultimate meaning or with corrupting convictions—here, too, a panacea has turned out to be a problem. What quality of faith and character is going to use our educated minds? Now in my elder years, there-

fore, I am even more convinced than I was at the beginning that the truths about God and man, about right and wrong, for which the Christian gospel stands are man's indispensable necessity. Insofar as that idea has used me—I am grateful.[1]

The Church and Higher Education

Sensing from the beginning the importance of a religious dimension to education, the churches in America founded schools from coast to coast. As a rule these were pioneering institutions, built on the edge of a moving frontier. Mainly they were elementary and secondary schools, many of which have disappeared completely from the scene. Others became colleges and universities. Most of the great private colleges of our day were founded by the churches.

Some state institutions of early days were the direct product of equally strong religious conviction. Thus the University of Michigan was granted a charter in 1817 as the result of efforts by a Catholic priest, a Protestant minister, and a territorial judge. The university had for many years printed across the platform of its assembly hall these famous words from the Ordinance of 1787, which created the Northwest Territory:

> Religion, morality, and knowledge being necessary to good government and the happiness of mankind, schools and the means of education shall forever be encouraged.

Today the churches have developed at public institutions Christian centers from which may emanate the

---

[1] Harry Emerson Fosdick, *The Living of These Days* (New York: Harper & Brothers, 1956), pp. 271-272.

insights of religious thought and the experience of meaningful worship, even though the institutions themselves are not church supported. We dare not underestimate the importance of these programs of service.

Through the years Christian men and women of little and of great wealth have given liberally to the support of Christian colleges. Their reasons for what were often sacrificial contributions are strikingly summarized in the words of Asa Candler, whose large gifts occasioned the moving of Emory University to Atlanta, and helped in its subsequent development:

> I am profoundly impressed that what our country needs is not more secularized education, but more of the education that is fundamentally and intentionally religious. I see no way by which such religious education can be supplied without institutions of learning owned and controlled by the churches.
>
> Boards of trustees that are independent of all government must inevitably change in person and policy with the changeful years. But the Church of God is an enduring institution; it will live when individuals and secular corporations have perished. It is not easily carried about by the shifting winds of doctrine which so affect men and institutions too responsive to the transient modes of thought and custom which come and go with the seasons.
>
> Hence, I desire that whatever I am able to invest in the work of education shall be ministered by the Church, with a definite and continuous religious purpose.

Institutional Tradition To begin with, every faculty member should understand fully the fundamental tradition of the institution he serves, including its religious heritage. This is to be found especially in the charter and history of the college. These documents almost invariably strike one as epics of sacrifice and service.

The liberal provisions of the charters of most colleges related to the churches today are also likely to prove surprising to the uninitiated. Only rarely were narrowly sectarian purposes envisioned or permitted. The actual point of view of pioneer church colleges was well summarized by Matthew Simpson, early president of what is now DePauw University:

> If by sectarianism is meant that any privilege shall be extended to a youth of one denomination above another or that the faculty shall endeavor to proselyte those placed under their instruction or dwell upon minor points controverted between the branches of the great Christian family, then there is not and we hope there never will be sectarianism here. But if by sectarianism is meant that professors are religious men and that they have settled views upon Christian character and duty then we ever hope to be sectarian.

The tradition of a college should be understood by its staff, and it should be respected. Its application may, of course, be modified and refined through the years.

Church and College But far more is expected of the teacher in a Christian college than the understanding of its tradition. It is also essential to appreciate the full possibility of church and college working in partnership.[2] The church is the necessary community of those who have been captivated by the love of God. It is,

[2] I am indebted for the remainder of this section to my colleague, Dr. Richard N. Bender.

fundamentally, a community of commitment, expressing its common life in corporate worship, in Christian nurture, and in co-operative Christian action. It is tangible evidence of the social interdependence of persons even for the fulfillment of their highest ideals. It is evidence also of the conviction that the love of God must express itself in and through human community. The church is called to be the "beloved community" through which personal and cultural reconciliation with God may be achieved.

If the church is to be this kind of fact in experience, a division of responsibility is necessary. Because the church is a human community, every specific example of it falls far short of the ideal to which it aspires. Every organized church must be clearly distinguished from the spiritual Church. The specific college falls far short, also, of the ideal of a true community of masters and scholars in quest of knowledge. Yet, to understand the church and the college and the unique relationship upon which they have entered, each must be seen against the perspective of what, at its best, it aspires to be.

The Christian college must be sustained by the fellowship, the prayers, and the service of the Christian church. No educational institution can exist in a vacuum. Its life must be supported by a productive alliance with a community of common concern. The Christian church is the only contemporary community whose own purposes and resources are capable of systematic support for an educational program in which the divine-human dimension is natural and essential.

There is another side to the coin. The church desperately needs the college. The church has been at its worst when it has lost the capacity of critical self-evaluation. Only a devoted community of free Christian scholarship can maintain the constructive self-criticism that protects against the incredible absurdities and immoralities at times perpetrated in the name of the Holy Spirit.

Another and perhaps even more essential need for which the church must depend on the college is cultural leadership which is at once skilled and devout. If the church takes seriously its role as mediator of the love of God to a culture seeking to recover meaning and direction, this kind of leadership is indispensable. Even the highest motives will be frustrated without technical competence. The church-related college must be one of the major instruments through which Christian commitment is linked to trained and disciplined abilities.

The church-related college is sustained and made relevant through its alliance with the Christian church. It renders to the church those services that only a scholarly community can provide. Its essential contribution to the higher educational world stems from its central intention to demonstrate the relevance of the divine-human dimension to the educational task.

The Spirit of the Teacher Thus teaching in a Christian college is an opportunity to link oneself with the purposes and inspiration of the Christian church. Here again the college is mainly dependent upon the commitment and spirit of the individual teacher.

Some years ago, in addressing the National Education Association, the Reverend Franklin Clark Fry of the United Lutheran Church reminded schoolteachers of the one vital approach to the problem of religion in public education. These are his words:

> There is only one good solution to the problem of religion in public education; there is even only one feasible solution of the present impasse. That is in you, in each one as an individual.
>
> The one attainable junction of these two supreme influences in the lives of young Americans that so often seem parallel and in tension, that act like strangers and often antagonists, is and must be in living personalities. There is only one integration of education and religion against which there is no constitution, no law; that is unanswerably right—and immensely persuasive. It is the vital integration in an educated and religious man.

Thou shalt love the Lord thy God with all thy mind.

This statement implies equally the profound responsibility of the teacher on a church-college campus. When the faculty are themselves truly committed, and witness to their faith through their work, the college may indeed become a community of seekers after truth in the best sense.

This does not mean, of course, that a teacher should become a preacher. Quite the contrary! A church or a chapel is the place for preaching; a classroom is the place for teaching. Yet the value system of the teacher will inevitably emerge if his teaching is vital. One is reminded of Alfred North Whitehead's reply to the question of what he taught: "I teach Whitehead I, Whitehead II, Whitehead III."

Education and Christian Values Does an education of highest academic standards in an atmosphere of faith make a difference? It is a question which must concern every teacher. His own study of results over the years may be the best evidence, but he must be alert to the observations of others.

A recent provocative attempt to evaluate the impact of general education in the social sciences upon the values of American students is highly discouraging. The author, a professor of political science at the University of Pennsylvania, came to the conclusion that student values change little as a result of general courses in the social sciences. The exceptions he found are, however, of impressive importance. The author notes that student values *do* change in college, in some instances substantially. Furthermore, "potency to affect student values is found in the distinctive climate of a few institutions, (and in) the individual and personal magnetism of a sensitive teacher with strong value-commitments of his own." [3] Obtaining teachers with strong commitments is the number-one problem of every college.

The Faculty Christian Fellowship Many teachers are for the first time becoming concerned about the religious and moral influences of higher education. This is by no means confined to teachers in church-related colleges. One important sign of the concern is the movement known as the Faculty

[3] Philip E. Jacob, *Changing Values in College* (New York: Harper & Brothers, 1957), p. 11.

Christian Fellowship, made up of men and women in every part of the country seeking to discover the role of the Christian faculty member in the college and university. Information about the Faculty Christian Fellowship may be obtained by writing to Dr. Richard N. Bender, P. O. Box 871, Nashville 2, Tenn.

The journal which represents current thought of Christian teachers is *The Christian Scholar,* published quarterly at 475 Riverside Drive, New York 27, New York. Every teacher today has available, therefore, new help in his own search for significance and in his efforts to make his teaching vital. But the task is not done. All teachers will understand the point of this editorial note in *The Christian Scholar:*

> We have some exploring to do—of our humane tradition, of the wealth of constructive thought which today can be brought to the service of the academic enterprise, of our various intellectual and theological distinctions, and of the opportunities which are ours in the colleges and universities today to find new ways to live on and break through the frontiers of a new and better day.[4]

The Marks of a Christian Teacher

What are the distinctive marks of a Christian teacher? No two statements would agree, and perhaps fortunately so. In a moving address at the First Convocation of Christian Colleges at Denison University in 1954, Dr. Marjorie Reeves of England outlined her view of the matter in the following striking way. These ideas merit closest study:

[4] *The Christian Scholar,* Vol. 40, No. 2, June, 1957.

I. Attitudes to Knowledge
   1. Fearless inquiry that follows the clue to truth wherever it leads, yet reverence for the fundamental mystery of the creation in all its manifestations.
   2. Humility with regard to our own capacity for knowing the truth, a sense of the partiality, relativity, and imperfection of all human knowledge, yet no cynicism with regard to the intrinsic value of the human effort to know.
   3. Openness to the impact of new truth and experience, to the reception of new insights and viewpoints, yet realization that we are called to commitment in conviction, in value-judgments, in belief as a basis for action, albeit the only commitment we can at a given moment make is an experimental one.

II. Attitudes to People
   1. Belief in the sanctity of persons and therefore reverence for their integrity.
   2. Eagerness to meet them in a full encounter which involves fundamental beliefs and attitudes, not a surface contact of minds alone.
   3. Willingness to know oneself in relation to others in the sense of learning when to lead and when to follow, remembering always that "ye are members one of another."

III. Attitudes to Society
   1. Recognition that the academic community depends on the labors of others—acknowledgment of the cost of scholarship in terms of human toil.
   2. Therefore, acceptance of responsibility of all who enjoy an academic life to serve their community.
   3. Yet acknowledgment continually of the higher loyalty, the heavenly citizenship, which has so often to be held in tension with the earthly.

Thus all our activity must be brought *sub specie aeternitatis,* and so we come to the place where all our human learning and action is seen to be partial and incomplete but significant—to the place where, being brought under obedience, we can command our powers most fully and send them speeding forth down the avenues of knowledge with a vigour and a joyfulness which belong only to "the service which is perfect freedom."

Perhaps all that has already been said regarding the teacher in the Christian college may be summed up in the following words of Ordway Tead:

> The teacher has to be helped to establish an orientation to the culture which transcends defensiveness, indifference, or despair, and exemplifies a faith, hope, and love which radiate through all his scholarly efforts.[5]

Responsibility and Opportunity

Every teacher thus bears a tremendous responsibility, both to himself and to his students. He is called, first *to be,* and then *to lead and guide.* His mission and responsibility are second to none; his opportunity is unmatched in other professions. As a member of a unique type of community, he can help to develop the kind of educational program and environment which will influence positively the whole intellectual atmosphere of the nation. This will be done first by setting an example, and second by helping to produce men and women of full-orbed power to meet the desperate needs of our times.

A student of the late Rufus Jones, inspired Quaker mystic, once said of him: "He lighted my candle." Can there be higher praise for a teacher?

[5] Ordway Tead, in *Improving College Instruction,* Fred J. Kelly, ed. (Washington, D. C.: American Council on Education).

Bibliography

The bibliography which follows is not in any sense comprehensive. It does, however, list some of the best books for the thoughtful teacher who wishes to evaluate his own goals and his progress toward them.

Sidney J. French, ed., *Accent on Teaching.* New York: Harper & Brothers, 1954. 334 pp. Twenty-five teachers in American colleges and universities explain their ideas of general education in the liberal arts.

Barzun, Jacques, *Teacher in America.* Boston: Little, Brown & Company, 1945, 321 pp. Teaching is a dramatic art, says the author, and unless a teacher recognizes this, he fails to excite his students. Education should send the student out on his own—to learn for himself. The book also treats the teaching of the various subjects in the curriculum.

Beach, Waldo, *Conscience on Campus.* New York: Association Press, 1958, 124 pp. A searching look at the problem of ethical anarchy on the campus. Highly stimulating.

Brown, Kenneth I., *Not Minds Alone—Some Frontiers of Christian Education.* New York: Harper & Brothers, 1954, 206 pp. The cause of Christian education is discussed in this volume, Christian education which meets all the qualitative and quantitative standards of sound academic education. It supports the educational view that education is not only for the mind, but for the heart as well.

Buxton, Claude E., *College Teaching: A Psychologist's View*. New York: Harcourt, Brace and Company, 1950, 404 pp. The title suggests the content of the book, a discussion of a large variety of technical problems.

Espy, R. H. Edwin, *The Religion of College Teachers: The Beliefs, Practices, and Religious Preparation of Faculty Members in Church-Related Colleges*. New York: Association Press, 1951, 216 pp. This book deals with the meaning of religion to the teacher in the church-related college and the place he gives it in his teaching.

Fairchild, Hoxie N., ed., *Religious Perspectives in College Teaching*. New York: The Ronald Press Company, 1952, 460 pp. A look at the various college disciplines and the perspectives some Christian teachers bring to them.

Ferré, Nels F. S., *Christian Faith and Higher Education*. New York: Harper & Brothers, 1954, 251 pp. A well-known Christian theologian examines urgent problems of higher education.

Gross, John O., *Education for Life*. New York: Abingdon Press, 1948, 219 pp. A vigorous statement of the possibilities of Christian higher education.

Harvard Education 1948: The Students' View. Cambridge, 1949, 77 pp. Here a strong case is made for student-oriented education at Harvard. Written soon *after* the celebrated Harvard Report.

Highet, Gilbert, *The Art of Teaching*. New York: Alfred A. Knopf, Inc., 1950, 291 pp. Teaching as an art is discussed by a noted classroom teacher and scholar. The broad attributes of a good teacher are described, with the human and common-sense approach stressed.

Justman, Joseph and Walter H. Mais, *College Teaching: Its Practice and Its Potential*. New York: Harper & Brothers, 1956, 257 pp. Here are discussed the principles and techniques of college teaching. Curriculum and the use of new instructional techniques are considered.

Paul Klapper, ed., *College Teaching*. Tarrytown-on-Hudson, N. Y.: World Book Company, 1920, 583 pp. This is a pioneering and provocative study of college teaching. Many concrete examples.

LeFevre, Perry D., *The Christian Teacher*. New York: Abingdon Press, 1958, 176 pp. The Christian teacher's concerns in higher education. A clarification of some of the ways in which the teacher may fulfill his calling.

Lowry, Howard F., *The Mind's Adventure*. Philadelphia: Westminster Press, 1950. 154 pp. The function of the Christian college and the educational issues of today are attractively treated here. Included are discussions of the influence of the church-related college in the past and its role in the future.

Marshall, Max S., *Two Sides to a Teacher's Desk*. New York: The Macmillan Company, 1951, 284 pp. Teachers and students are urged to be partners in the joint enterprise of education. Students will learn if the educational system only keeps out of their way.

Riley, John W., Jr., Bryce F. Ryan, and Marcia Lifshitz, *The Student Looks at His Teacher*. New Brunswick: Rutgers University Press, 1950, 166 pp. The students' views of their teachers are outlined in this volume.

Smith, Huston, *The Purposes of Higher Education*. New York: Harper & Brothers, 1955, 218 pp. Teachers of broadly divergent views deal with fundamental philosophical and educational ideas. Clear, concise, highly readable.

Townsend, Agatha, *College Freshmen Speak Out*. New York: Harper & Brothers, 1956, 136 pp. Student problems in the first college year are the subject of this book. The author suggests reasons as to why first-year work has not been more satisfactory, and offers suggestions as to how it may be made more meaningful and significant.

Umstattd, J. G., *Teaching Procedures Used in Twenty-Eight Midwestern and Southwestern Colleges and Universities*. Austin: Cooperative Society, Inc., 1954, 91 pp. Over a thousand teachers in many fields answered a questionnaire about their teaching practices, how these have changed during recent years, and what they consider ideal teaching conditions.